Chapter 1

Rob Lindsted: Welcome, Brother Earl Warner. One of the things I find so interesting about you is that you are a Hebrew Christian.

Earl Warner: That's right. I am a Hebrew instead of a Jewish Christian, because even though I was born and raised in an orthodox Jewish home, there is a slight technical difference between being Jewish and Hebrew. Jewish is really the religion of the people and Hebrew is the racial background. Consequently, I was born and raised in an orthodox Jewish home. I became a believer in Jesus Christ at the age of 28. At that time I became a Hebrew Christian.

Rob Lindsted: We want to get into your testimony. You are so familiar with Israel, being a Hebrew Christian. You have spent a lifetime studying the Bible and its prophecies. You spent eleven years with Midwest Hebrew Ministries. Now you are holding seminars and conferences all over the country. We have a common bond in that we both are looking for the soon return of Jesus Christ.

We want to talk about a number of subjects. With each of these subjects we want to inform our readers how we can please God in these last days. I really believe that we are living in the last days and we need to be living our lives in such a way that we anticipate the return of Christ. And at the same time we want to be a faithful witness. I think there are a number of people that will get some keen insight not only into end-time Bible prophecy, but also how to be a testimony to others who are Jewish. I would like to begin with how the Lord saved you.

Earl Warner: Actually, I came to hear the gospel out of curiosity. I never really heard the gospel, or if I did I don't recall. I didn't know what a Hebrew Christian was. I had never heard a Hebrew Christian speak. I went to a Jewish synagogue to hear Dr. Hyman Appleman speak. I don't remember what text he used at that time, but what he said seemed to make sense to me. At the end of the service he had every eye closed and every head bowed and he invited anyone in the audience who wanted to be saved to raise their hand. Well, at this time I wanted to be saved but I didn't really want to raise my hand, but it seemed like a power stronger than my own forced me to raise my hand. Then he invited all those who had raised their hands to stand up, and then to talk to him after the meeting. That was the time when I actually became a believer in Christ as my Savior.

It was quite a situation because I am the youngest of twelve. Being raised in an orthodox Jewish home, when an orthodox Jewish person converts to another religion, quite often the family will have a funeral service for that individual. The more affluent ones will probably have a casket, the rabbi, the burial, everything except a body in the casket. We were quite poor. My mother and father at this time were living in California. I don't know if they had the funeral for me; I wasn't invited. But that is how I came to be a believer in Christ.

Rob Lindsted: Being raised in an orthodox Jewish home, the night you attended that service would your parents have been violently opposed to your attending that service?

Earl Warner: Yes, they would have been.

Rob Lindsted: Were there other Jews there, or was it a case of there were just other people there and that is why you decided to go?

Earl Warner: I heard about this man being there, and out of curiosity I went. I don't know if there were any other Jewish people there. There may have been.

Rob Lindsted: Other times during your life as you heard of people who believed that Jesus was the Messiah, that He had died and been resurrected, what were your thoughts?

Earl Warner: I really never heard much about the resurrection of Jesus. Any time the name of Jesus was mentioned, at least in my own experience, it was anathema to me. I never realized that one day that would be the most wonderful of all names to me. I never heard much about the resurrection of Jesus except when my parents would talk about something way off in the future. They did not believe that Jesus was the Messiah. Of course, we know as we get into the Scriptures exactly how Messiah was to be identified and how Christ fulfilled each and every one of these prophecies. I believe with all my heart that He is the Messiah.

Rob Lindsted: You are the youngest of twelve children, so as your family heard that the baby brother had left the Jewish faith and embraced Christianity, what kind of reaction did you get from your brothers and sisters?

Earl Warner: Well, it wasn't very good. I didn't tell my family for about three months after I became a believer because quite often they have those funeral services. One Sunday morning, as I was sitting in church, the Spirit of God really convicted me that I had to tell my family. My mother and father by this time were living in California, along with about half my brothers and sisters. I called one of my sisters after I came home from church that Sunday morning. I asked my sister if she would be good enough to call the others and ask them to come to her house.

I took my Bible and started to plan my approach to my family. I didn't know what I was going to say to them because I really was not ready to do this. As I was trying to think of what to say to my family, my mind was empty. I just couldn't think at all. I opened my Bible at random and it opened to Mark 13. My eyes seemed to drop to one verse, verse 11. There I read, *"But when they shall lead you, and deliver you up, take no thought beforehand what ye shall speak, neither do ye premeditate: but whatsoever shall be given you in that hour, that speak ye: for it is not ye that speak, but the Holy Ghost."* And I knew that verse was for me. The Lord spoke through me at that time and answered some questions for me that I could never have answered. I wouldn't want to go through it again, but I got an idea of what Daniel went through in the lion's den.

When my brothers and sisters began to come in, we all got together in the living room of my sister's home. When we were ready to speak they realized something wasn't quite kosher there that afternoon. I had learned a couple of great Old Testament messianic verses that had been a great help to me. One is Isaiah 7:14: *"Therefore the Lord himself shall give you a sign; Behold, a virgin shall conceive, and bear a son, and shall call his name Immanuel."* I told my family I believe this is the way Messiah had to be born because our own prophets indicated Messiah had to be born of a virgin. I told them this is the way Messiah was to be born into the world and Christ was the only one born this way, so He must be the Messiah. Then I quoted Isaiah 9:6 *"For unto us a child is born, unto us a son is given: and the government shall be upon his shoulder: and his name shall be called Wonderful, Counsellor, The mighty God, The everlasting Father, The Prince of Peace."* This indicates that this baby was the mighty God. To me that is a very precious truth, that Christ was not only a man as we are but that He was God manifested in the flesh. I told them that we Jewish people should be the first to acknowledge this one as our Messiah and Savior according to our own Hebrew prophets.

This went on for three hours. At the end of that three-hour period, when they recognized the fact they couldn't get me to denounce Christ, one of my sisters told me that if I wanted to believe this way, that was fine, but not to tell my parents because it would kill them. I said, "Molly, if you saw a newspaper advertising bacon for ten cents a pound, would you tell Annabelle so she could get bacon for ten cents a pound too?" She said, "Sure." I said, "This is what I'm doing here today. I know something I want you to know about. I know something you need to know."

Rob Lindsted: There is no doubt that, even then, God was preparing you for the work He would have you doing in the Midwest Hebrew Ministries where you would have the opportunity to present the gospel to both Jews and Christians. I believe that God has used your background as an orthodox Jewish person to help you understand exactly what the Bible is saying and then to see the fulfillment in these last days. As a Jewish person, what do you really see in terms of the fulfillment of prophecy as we live in this day and time concerning the nation of Israel?

Earl Warner: I believe it is a fulfillment of dozens of Old Testament scriptures concerning the land, concerning the fact that these people would be restored to the land in the latter days. We have not seen that completely fulfilled, but we have seen the beginning of that because God has indicated that this land would be theirs and this is the place where God would restore them to.

I really believe that on May 14, 1948, Israel became a nation for the first time since they went into Babylonian captivity. I believe that Israel is in the land today only because God is keeping His promise and because of His grace.

There are three great groups of Jewish people as far as religions is concerned: the orthodox, the conservative, and the liberal. The liberal, or reformed, really don't believe much about the Old Testament, but the orthodox have a great interest and desire to go back to the Holy Land and see the temple rebuilt. The fact is that God has allowed many Jewish people to go back into that land in spite of all obstacles; they are coming back into the land today. They have not been able to do so before 1948.

Rob Lindsted: We have seen literally tens of thousands of Russian Jews come back to Israel. I know this has a special meaning for you.

Earl Warner: My mother came from Russia.

Rob Lindsted: I was looking at the passage in Ezekiel 38, and among the things I noticed was that when Rosh, or Russia, comes down against Israel, they come down to take a prey, they come down to take a spoil for food and money, and then it also says for people. I can't help but wonder if maybe they are not going to come back and claim those people that left Russia really belong to Russia after all. Even though they are going to be transplanted into Israel, I just wonder if, the way it is worded here, this is just one more indicator that we are living very near the time that Russia will make her move. I think that will take place after the Rapture.

As you talk to other Jews and as you share your faith in Jesus Christ, do they respond at all to prophecy? Is that a good way to witness to Jewish people?

Earl Warner: Quite often that depends on if the person is orthodox, conservative, or reformed. When speaking to an orthodox person, I like to use the Old Testament scriptures and show what God has promised. When I speak with reformed Jewish people, they do not believe the Old Testament, and the New Testament as well, as the Word of God. I use logic with them and tell them because he and I are Jewish people and we are still in existence today, it definitely shows us that the Bible is the Word of God, because it is the promise that God has made. If God has made those promises and is keeping those promises today, definitely this is the Word of God.

Rob Lindsted: Concerning these promises that God made to Abraham as a Hebrew Christian, you can say, "These are promises that our fathers and our grandfathers counted on, and we are seeing them fulfilled." That has to be a powerful message to those that are raised with the Old Testament as being the truth of God.

Earl Warner: They cannot deny these things. When we see Israel back in the land that God promised them, surely it is the fulfillment of God's Word. They cannot deny it. It is logic.

Chapter 2

Rob Lindsted: Basically there are three main groups of Jewish people. What is the distinction to what each of these believe?

Earl Warner: The three groups are orthodox, conservative, and reformed. The orthodox Jews are those who are very religious. In fact, the orthodox man will attend synagogue services every morning and every evening. My father spent hours each day reading the Scriptures and praying. If they are not able to go to a synagogue because of health or whatever, they are obligated under the Mosaic law to say their prayers. They are supposed to do this every day. On some of our trips to Israel, after the plane has gotten up and leveled off, a number of the Jewish people got up in the aisle and had the services right there in the morning. The orthodox people won't turn a light on or off during that time. They won't answer a telephone. They are not allowed to carry any money with them during that time.

The conservatives are quite religious, but not nearly so much as the orthodox people are. The orthodox Jew does accept the Old Testament as inspired of God, whereas the conservative will accept at least the five books of Moses as inspired of God (some will accept more).

The reformed, or liberal, Jewish people accept the Old Testament Scriptures as good literature or history, but not necessarily as the Word of God. They will quite often work on Saturday, their Sabbath. They consider it just another day.

Rob Lindsted: We see almost a parallel in our own country. We see so many that claim to be Christians, and some really study the Bible, they believe the whole Bible. Another group remind me of the conservative group. They believe some of the Bible. Then, of course, there are so many who show up at Easter and Christmas. They really believe the Bible is just a good story. I see three divisions in thinking in America almost parallel to the Jewish people that you've described.

Let's say that we were visiting an orthodox home where they accept the whole Old Testament as being the inspired Word of God. Would they look at these verses that we do concerning the coming of Messiah, if they don't accept Jesus as Messiah? How do they deal with those verses?

Earl Warner: I've talked to rabbis about that. In fact, I have a nephew who is an orthodox rabbi. In discussing Isaiah 7:14, one orthodox rabbi told me that the word for "virgin" in the Hebrew is *almah*, which means young maiden, but not necessarily a virgin. But this word is only used of a young woman who is a virgin, indicating that a young woman who was a virgin would give birth to a son. One rabbi said that he felt that that was going to be one of the sons of Isaiah the prophet. I said, "Rabbi, how could it be anything but the miracle, because God said He would give them a sign." It is no sign when a young girl of 12 or 14 gives birth to a child, and this is happening all the way through. It is a sign, a miracle, that God Himself is going to perform. Then when we come into the New Testament we find this is exactly what did happen — a virgin gave birth to a Son. That was the miracle that God had promised.

Rob Lindsted: The people that we see at the Western Wall, would those be the orthodox Jews then?

Earl Warner: Yes. Actually those at the Western Wall are the ultra-orthodox Jewish people.

Rob Lindsted: It appears to me that the orthodox Jew would be the first to recognize that Jesus is the Messiah because they accept all of the Old Testament, whereas the reformed Jews see this as some good information, or maybe some laws of our ancestors. Are orthodox Jews more open to the gospel?

Earl Warner: I personally would rather speak to an orthodox Jewish person than to a reformed. The reformed Jew does not accept the Old Testament as the Word of God, whereas the rabbi will accept the Old Testament as inspired. But they don't have the same interpretation of the messianic references that we do. Many of the messianic references speak of Christ, which means Messiah. To us these references are very meaningful because they were fulfilled by the Lord Jesus Christ; the orthodox Jewish people do not believe that. But because it is in the Old Testament, and they do accept the Old Testament as inspired, I am able to speak of the Scriptures which they accept. And even though many of these do not accept what we are trying to teach them, at least it is the Word of God that they are getting. Of course, this is the important thing.

Rob Lindsted: Several years ago there was a man at the Midwest Hebrew

Ministries conference who came to me right after lunch. He said he was a Jewish fellow that had been brought there by another university student and at that conference he accepted Christ. Just this year I met another fellow, a Gentile, and as far as I can tell both men were saved at the same conference. It is amazing that these orthodox Jews who are so intent against Jesus being the Messiah really might be the most open to it. I think of this in terms of the great passage in Matthew where it says the gospel of the kingdom will go throughout the world during the Tribulation, and then the passage in Revelation where the 144,000 evangelists are mentioned. I think they are going to be Jewish, and it appears that they could possibly be orthodox Jews, because maybe these will be the very people that will accept the news that Jesus is the Messiah.

Earl Warner: I agree with you. In fact, I believe the 144,000 are living today because I believe the Rapture of the Church is so near. These 144,000 ave to be living today if they are going to evangelize during the Tribulation. They are going to preach like we have never heard preaching before.

Rob Lindsted: This brings to mind several questions, one of which is: Is a Jewish person saved because the person is Jewish?

Earl Warner: I wish I could say yes to that, but I can't because the Bible doesn't teach that. The Jewish nation is saved. In other words, it will never be destroyed or annihilated because God made that promise, but the individual Jewish person has to come to the place where he or she believes in the fact that the Lord Jesus Christ came and died for them, and that they must too accept Him as Savior.

Rob Lindsted: So you are telling me that a Jew and a Gentile are saved exactly the same way?

Earl Warner: Amen, brother.

Rob Lindsted: This is a very important principle, because I find confusion concerning that. I really believe that this is why the message of the gospel of Jesus Christ is suitable to be preached to both Gentile and Jew. And yet, it is a matter of us taking a different perspective for the Jew to show that Jesus does satisfy the claims of the Old Testament, and for the Gentile it may be a different logic process involved. But in both cases it does require faith in the finished work of Jesus Christ.

Another thing I find fascinating is the idea of thirteen principles of Jewish faith. Would you share some of these with us?

Earl Warner: I might say that these were formulated by a man named Moses Mamambre, who lived about the twelfth century.

Rob Lindsted: So these have been around awhile. Would these principles be well known to a Jew in America, or would it be more the orthodox Jew that would be familiar with these thirteen principles?

Earl Warner: More the orthodox Jewish person. I'm sure some of the reformed Jews don't know anything about it. But the orthodox Jewish person, at least the head of the house, will recite them on a daily basis.

You will find that these principles coincide with what we as Christians believe. One of them is: *"I believe with perfect faith that the Creator, blessed be His name, is Author and God of everything that has been created, and that He has made, does make, and will make all things."* We know that this is true. In several scriptures in the New Testament we find that the Lord Jesus Christ, who is God made flesh, is the one who created the earth, the sea, and all things therein.

Another one: *"I believe with perfect faith that the Creator, blessed be His name, is a Unity, and that there is no unity in any manner like unto His, and that He alone is our God who was, is, and will be."* The greatest prayer the Jewish people have is found in Deuteronomy 6:4: *"Hear, O Israel: The Lord our God is one Lord."* The word for "one" has the idea of more than one, composing one. For example, the twelve tribes of Israel compose the one nation. That is the word that God used in that particular prayer, indicating that there is a Trinity. We find that in the very first verse of the Bible.

Rob Lindsted: That is interesting, because all along God taught them concerning one God, yet also the plural aspects of the Trinity. I've always thought it was interesting that from the time He introduced Abraham, Isaac, and Jacob how often He refers to Himself as the God of Abraham, Isaac, and Jacob. What a great picture of the Trinity. Jacob shows the great work of the Holy Spirit; Isaac is the great example of the work of the Son, especially in the sacrifice mentioned in Genesis 22; and Abraham, of course, is a picture of the Father. So while they show wording that would allow for a Triune Godhead, it was still one God. I don't see a single thing that a Christian couldn't adhere to in that principle.

Earl Warner: In all thirteen principles, actually, except one. And part of that one applies as well. In all of these principles we can see a lot of what the Jewish people believe, and how we Christians believe almost the exact same thing that an orthodox Jewish person believes.

Rob Lindsted: As we look at those principles, let's say that you were to have a conversation with an orthodox Jewish person. Could these principles perhaps be used to introduce him to the very fact that as we accept the Bible and as we accept Jesus Christ, we don't think there is a single thing violated in those principles, at least in general terms. Would this be an effective way to talk to them?

Earl Warner: I think it would be very effective. They will understand that we as Christians uphold the very same doctrines and teachings as they do, with one exception: that my Jewish brethren are still waiting for Messiah to come; we believe He has come in the person of the Lord Jesus Christ because He has fulfilled the 333 Old Testament messianic references concerning His coming. He must and is, as I believe, the true Messiah who came 2,000 years ago, but who is going to come again to take us unto Himself.

Rob Lindsted: This is fascinating. Name just a few signs of the emminent Rapture of the Church, especially those that relate to Israel itself.

Earl Warner: Well, I think the fact that Israel is a nation again for the first time in all these years is distinct proof to us that the Lord is coming, because this was to take place in the last days. In Hosea 3, we find that Israel shall be without a king, without a prince, and so forth, for many years. Afterward, she shall be brought back into the land. The fact is that Israel hasn't had a king since the Babylonian captivity. And there won't be a king on that throne until King Jesus. This just gladdens my heart.

Rob Lindsted: In that same passage in Hosea it mentions that they will be without a sacrifice, and we know that since 70 A.D. there has been no sacrifice and no temple, and yet the Bible is very clear that in the middle of the Tribulation the Antichrist will stop the sacrifice. I believe that as we see the activity that is going on in Israel, we see the preparations being made for sacrificial worship. That is a great sign that the Lord has allowed us to see being fulfilled

Chapter 3

Rob Lindsted: Russia has been in the news a lot recently. We read alot about the Cold War being over and the friendship that is developing between the United States and Russia. Yet as I go to the Bible, I can't help but warn people that the Bible says that before it is all done, Russia is going to invade Israel. I know that to many people this seems like such a controversial idea, but today we want to talk about Russia and her future, and how this is related to Israel. How is this received among Jewish people?

Earl Warner: In Ezekiel 38 and 39, we find Russia and many of her allied nations coming down against Israel in the future. In fact, I believe this is probably the next great biblical war to be fought. In fact, Moshe Dyan, who was a great general of Israel during the 1940s, indicated that the next great war Israel would have would be against Russia. Even though Russia has never come against Israel in the past, they will come against them in the future.

This almost came to pass in 1982 when Israel sent their army into Lebanon to push back the PLO. The PLO were lobbing shells into the northern settlements of Israel. Some of their ambassadors were being slain in other parts of the world and Israel had to do something about it. They sent their army up and drove them back to Beirut. When they came to Sidon, about 25 miles north of the Lebanese border, they found under the town the world's largest armory, all full of Russian war equipment. In one of the rooms they found enough coffee beans to float a battleship. In another room the found documents written in the Russian language that Russia intended to invade Israel and the Middle East on August 4, 1982. Israel went there in June of 1982, not really knowing what was in these tunnels.

Rob Lindsted: So they suspected that there was a plan of Russia to invade Israel, but they just didn't know the date. Once these documents were discovered, we could have been possibly two months away from this passage in Ezekiel 38 being fulfilled. I guess all we can say is that it wasn't the Lord's timing yet, because we know that this is going to take place. It is just a matter of when.

You mentioned that Moshe Dyan believed that Russia will invade Israel. Did he get this belief from the passage in Ezekiel 38?

Earl Warner: I don't know if he got this information from the Bible or not, but he did recognize the fact that when the Arab armies came against Israel in 1948, all their equipment came from Russia.

Rob Lindsted: Jewish people accept the story concerning the Lebanon situation in 1982. But that story never made it to the press in America the way it should have, and it is almost a mystery why it didn't. That is the kind of thing that reporters seem to thrive on, but that story never really made it to the press, at least to the magnitude I would have expected. I checked this story out with a number of Jewish people in Israel. Every one of them can repeat this story in some fashion, that this is exactly why Israel had to invade Lebanon in 1982.

Earl Warner: They do believe that the next great war will be against Russia. My mother came from Russia, and I've known many fine Russian people. Many of them fail to realize that Russia will come down against Israel.

When is this going to take place? I believe it will take place after the Rapture of the Church has taken place. In 1 Thessalonians 4, Paul wrote that the Lord Himself is going to descend from Heaven with a shout and the dead in Christ will be raised up first; those who are living at that time too shall be caught up with Him. This is called the Rapture. This is going to take place before Russia and her allied nations come down because we read in Ezekiel 38:8,11, and 14 that the Jewish people are going to come from all over the world and will be at peace at that time. Now we know that Israel today is not at peace. In fact, Israel is probably more prepared for war than any other country in the world that is not actually at war right now.

Rob Lindsted: We have seen in our travels to their country that they have the best security for arrival into their country. If there is any country in the world that is really ready for war, on 24-hour-alert, it is Israel. But you are right. As we look at Ezekiel 38 it appears that they are at a time of peace, which indicates that a peace treaty must have been signed.

Earl Warner: With the Antichrist. It will be a false peace, to be sure. I really don't believe there will be any true peace in Israel until the Prince of Peace, the Lord Jesus Christ, comes down and brings peace to the world. This will be, of course, after the Tribulation Period. I believe that Russia and her satellite nations are going to come down into the Middle East to take a spoil. I think the spoil that Russia will be after will be the chemicals in the Dead Sea. I read somewhere that the total wealth from the chemicals in the Dead Sea would be more than the total wealth of the United States, France, and Great Britain put together. That would be an immense amount of money.

There is also the possibility that the spoil will be oil, which Andy SoRelle is currently trying to locate.

Rob Lindsted: You know, not only is Andy SoRelle still looking for oil there, but I know of three or four groups that are intensely looking for oil. Some believe that there are large pools of oil there. Time will tell if indeed Israel will be blessed of God with the natural resource of oil. Maybe the spoil they are coming to take will be oil; maybe it will be the wealth of the Dead Sea. But whatever it is, Russia is going to come for money. Lately as we have watched the news we have seen that Russia is desperate for money. So this would make a good time frame for that.

Earl Warner: It very well could take place, although the main thrust of Russia coming down against Israel will take place after the Rapture. But right now, as you mentioned, Russia does need oil and food. In fact, Russia was at one time the greatest oil-producing nation in the world. But their oil wells are running dry and they have commitments to many countries to supply them with oil. They can't do that now. So if Israel does find oil, it is very likely that Russia will invade her.

Rob Lindsted: Maybe we are seeing the time frame of God, because we have seen how the invasion into Lebanon actually prevented Russia from coming down into Israel in 1982, obviously not God's timeframe. This invasion can't take place until after the church is gone, becuase it is clear that they will be at peace. This condition will only be found in the first part of the Tribulation period.

As we look at this passage, I find another very interesting idea. It says when they come down *"To take a spoil, and to take a prey; to turn thine hand upon the desolate places that are now inhabited, and upon the people that are gathered out of the nations, which have gotten cattle and goods, that dwell in the midst of the land"* (Ezek. 38:12). It appears to me that they also come down because there are some people there of special interest. I just wonder if that could be the Russian people that are leaving Russia right now to settle in Israel, and if there will be a great turnaround. In other words, if these people were starting to be blessed in terms of their wealth, maybe Russia is going to say, "You owe us. After all, you are really part of us." Perhaps this is a playing out of God's final chapter. Until I had seen all these Russian people streaming into Israel, I had never thought of that.

As we look at where we are right now in terms of God's chronology in Bible prophecy, what would you say to someone who asked how you know that this is modern-day Russia? What are the indications that we have?

Earl Warner: We read in several places in Ezekiel 38 that the country of the northernmost parts is going to come down. If a person put their finger on a globe of the world, starting at Israel and going straight north, the northernmost part is Russia. There is no doubt about this.

In 1917, Russia became a superpower. About five years later, the U.S.S.R. was formed. Since that time, Russia has been a great enemy of the Jewish people. After Israel became a nation and sided with the allies of the United States, Russia really began to hate Israel more and more. I believe that Russia is the country that is mentioned here in Ezekiel 38. Another interesting point is that some of these countries that are going to come down with Russia were, until a few years ago, friendly with Israel.

Rob Lindsted: This is a marvelous indicator that we must be living in the last days. To me this says that we are living on the brink of Christ's coming for those that have accepted Him.

If we were to take these things, would it be reasonable to talk to an orthodox Jew concerning Ezekiel 38 and convince them that maybe we are living in the last days based on the scriptures concerning Russia? Is that a reasonable thing to do?

Earl Warner: I think so, because an orthodox Jewish person does believe the Old Testament is the Word of God. When they see something like this in the Bible, they cannot reject it.

Rob Lindsted: As we see all these things, I really believe that we are living in the last days.

Chapter 4

Rob Lindsted: As we look at the first coming of the Lord to this earth, how can we say that it is a fulfillment of Bible prophecy?

Earl Warner: There are 333 Old Testament messianic prophecies concerning the coming of Christ. He fulfilled each and every one of those. In Isaiah 7:14 we find that He had to come into the world in a certain way — He had to be born of a virgin. In Matthew 1 we find that the angel of the Lord told Joseph that she had conceived of the Holy Spirit in fulfillment of Isaiah 7:14. We find in Micah 5:2 exactly where He was to be born — Bethlehem of Judea. In Matthew 2 we find that is exactly where he was born. We find that He had to do certain types of ministering while He was on earth. All of these were fulfilled by the Lord while He was on this earth. But He also had to die. The reason for His death is given to us in Isaiah 53. God is going to lay upon Him all of our sins. That is fulfilled in the New Testament. Then we also find in the Old Testament that it had to come at a certain time. In Galatians 4:4 Paul wrote that when the fulness of time came God sent forth a Son made of a woman to redeem those under the law. He also had to die a certain kind of death. He could not die any other way than the way He did die. When you see all these things it just makes you rejoice over and over that the whole Bible is the Word of God.

Rob Lindsted: The aspect that is so unique is that God predicted these things concerning Christ. So why are the Jewish people not responding to Jesus as Savior?

Earl Warner: One of the rabbis to whom I spoke said that Jesus could not be the Messiah because when Messiah comes He is going to bring peace to the world. Christ did not do that when He came; consequently He cannot be the Messiah. We Christians do believe that Christ is God manifest in the flesh. This is taught over and over in the Bible. That doctrine is repugnant to the Jewish people. They do not believe that God would come to earth in the form of a man. They believe Messiah is going to be one who is going to come as a powerful, charismatic political person, but not a Divine being. The Jewish people fail to realize that Jesus is the one that the prophets wrote about. As an example, in Deuteronomy 18:15-18 we find that God told Moses, who in turn told the Jewish people that He was going to choose from out of the twelve tribes a prophet like unto Moses and that God was going to require the people to hearken unto Him. When the Lord was upon this earth He was asked many times by the people, "Are you that prophet?" So they do accept some things concerning the Messiah, but they fail to realize that Jesus is the Messiah.

Rob Lindsted: So what we are seeing is that the Bible is very clear concerning the Messiah. But they just can't picture the one who would be their King, their grand Savior having come the first time to die. What about His resurrection? Is this a problem to the Jewish person?

Earl Warner: The orthodox Jewish people do believe in resurrection. The liberal Jews don't. One of the thirteen principles of the orthodox Jews is, *"I believe with perfect faith in the fact that there will be a resurrection of the dead at the time when it shall please the Creator, blessed be His name."* The orthodox Jewish people do believe in the resurrection of the dead, whereas the reformed Jews do not. They believe that once a person dies, that person ceases to exist. Of course, that is far from the truth.

Rob Lindsted: This debate is not a new one. We read in the gospels even in the days of Jesus one of the things the Sadducees and the Pharisees argued about was the resurrection of the dead. Anyone who doesn't believe in the resurrection has a right to be sad because 1 Corinthians 15 is so clear that if Christ be not raised from the dead, then we are still in our sins. So this is a powerful doctrine. The Christian faith is totally unique in this. So the first coming of Christ is really a grand study of prophecy. It is a grand study of the Old Testament being fulfilled explicitly by Jesus Christ.

Now, let us talk about things that are in the future. What would be some of the outstanding passages that come to your mind concerning Israel in Bible prophecy, especially ones that we can put our finger on today and see they are being fulfilled?

Earl Warner: We read in Jeremiah 23, and Ezekiel 36 and 37 that Israel was going to be restored to the land in the latter days. As we go through Bible history we find that there were Hittites, Philistines, Jebusites, and so forth, that were enemies of Israel and not one of those countries is in existence today. Down through the years, the old Devil has tried to destroy Israel to prove himself stronger than God. God indicated this would never happen.

As we go through the book of Genesis, we find that God made a covenant with Abraham that Abraham's seed would be slaves in a land which was not theirs for 400 years and after that they would be brought out of the land of bondage, Egypt, and into the Promised Land. This in itself is just a tremendous miracle because they could not have done what they did without God's help. So we find that in these days in which we are living Israel is brought back to that land, not because they are bigger or better than anyone else, but because God is keeping His promise.

The greatest miracle to me regarding Israel today is the fact that in 1948, when Israel became a nation, there were only 600,000 total Jewish men, women, and children. Many of these came from Nazi Europe and were able to get into Israel by hook or crook. Many were disabled or elderly. England had the mandate over Palestine to make a homeland for the Jewish people and refused them the right to train any military forces. Yet these people, without any aircraft or heavy war equipment, overcame six trained armies. To me it is a miracle.

Rob Lindsted: It is amazing when you say they defeated six armies and they they didn't even have an army at that time. But they did have the promises of God.

You brought up an interesting point that Satan has tried to destroy Israel. Satan knew that the Messiah would come out of Israel, so all the way back in the book of Genesis when God promises that out of a woman there is going to come a Savior, he right away tried to destroy the human race. Later, when God makes the promise to Abraham, notice how Satan is always there trying to wipe out any chance of a Messiah. I just wonder if maybe this isn't why we see the work of Satan so strong against Israel, because he saw Israel getting in position to be reborn as a nation. I think this is why the Holocaust took place. I think it was Satan trying to wipe out the prospect of Israel being reborn. Every time Satan tries to wipe out the plan of salvation, God always has a way to bring it back. Maybe this is why we see so much persecution going on with regard to the nation of Israel.

If we were to talk to a Jew, other than Israel being back in the land, what would be another great biblical sign of Bible prophecy being fulfilled?

Earl Warner: I have been to Israel a number of times. The first bus ride that we took to Egypt from Israel is actually what we see fulfilled in Isaiah 35 — the desert shall blossom like the rose — in the Israeli Sinai Desert. It amazes me that as we went through that desert the ground was just like a beautiful garden. On the Egyptian side, what we saw there was exactly what we had expected a desert to be. It is just tremendous the things that are taking place in Israel. As I understand it, they are now exporting their fruits and vegetables to about sixty different countries around the world.

Rob Lindsted: These are great indicators of end-time prophetic Bible fulfillment. As I see these things, this is not just a message for Jews but for Gentiles as well. I really believe it is important for us to clearly understand that these are signs given by God in the Old Testament hundreds of years ago. None of these have been written in the last nineteen hundred years, yet as you mentioned, we are the ones seeing these things fulfilled. We can only pray that God will use this to wake up the hearts of people, both Jew and Gentile, that they might see we are living in the last days.

Chapter 5

Rob Lindsted: We are going to be looking at a subject that I think has caused so much confusion — the second coming of Christ and the fact that there are two aspects of it. Would you help us understand God's prophetic program that is ahead for us?

Earl Warner: Before I became a believer in Christ I didn't know a thing about the Messiah. I certainly didn't believe that He was going to come to this earth as He did. I didn't believe in that which is called the Rapture of the Church, the fact that He is going to take us up to be with Him in the glory and that He is going to come again and sit on David's throne. I knew nothing of those things until I became a believer in Christ. And then these things became very powerful to me. It became one of the most important subjects in the Scriptures to me. After I became a believer in Christ and began to read and study, I recognized the fact that the Lord said He was going to come again.

In the Old Testament, Daniel 12, we read that in the latter days knowledge is going to increase, and people shall go to and fro. This century began with a very limited use of electricity. There were no airplanes in the skies; there were no radios; there were no televisions. None of these things were in use at the beginning of this century. So many things are happening today.

We read about the coming of the Lord for His own. In John 14:2-3 Jesus said, *"In my Father's house are many mansions: if it were not so, I would have told you. I go to prepare a place for youa. And if I go and prepare a place for you, I will come again, and receive you unto myself; that where I am, there ye may be also."* This truth is foreign to the Jewish people. They don't believe that. They don't accept it. Yet this is taught in the Scriptures.

I believe very strongly that there is going to be a Messiah and that He is going to come down. During Passover, toward the end someone will get up and open the door. Everyone at the table stands up and faces that door. They then offer prayers and invite Elijah to come in and tell them when Messiah is going to come, failing to realize that Messiah did come 2,000 years before, in the person of the Lord Jesus Christ. They fail to recognize that, yet when you get into the New Testament, the book of Matthew for example, is still under the law. Even though Matthew is in the New Testament it is written on Old Testament ground. The Church has not yet begun; it doesn't begin until Acts 2. But we read in Matthew 24 that the disciples asked the Lord, "When are you going to come again? Give us a sign. Tell us when certain things are going to be." As we read some of these events which are going to take place in Matthew 24, we find that some of these events actually have to take place before the Lord comes again with His own.

The Second Coming of Christ is really in two aspects. The first aspect is when He comes for His own. He is not coming to the earth at that time. He will catch us up, the dead in Christ and those that are living at that time, and we will be caught up to be with the Lord forever. That is the first resurrection. Then the seven-year Tribulation Period takes place, and at the end of that seven-year period we will come down with Him to rule and reign with Him on this earth for 1,000 years. During that time Satan will have been cast into the bottomless pit. There are 333 Old Testament prophecies concerning the first coming of the Lord; there are about 1,800 concerning the second coming of the Lord, so we know that is yet to take place.

The Old Testament doesn't teach a whole lot about the Rapture of the Church. In fact, hardly anything. This is because it is a mystery. This is something in which the church is going to participate and is really the greatest experience we could possibly have when we are caught up to be with the Lord in glory. But the Old Testament does teach that the Messiah is going to come and rule and reign on David's throne. As an example, in Zechariah 14:16 we read, *"And it shall come to pass, that every one that is left of all the nations which came against Jerusalem shall even go up from year to year to worship the King, the Lord of hosts, and to keep the feast of tabernacles."* This king is none other than the Lord Jesus Christ. In Zechariah 12 we find some interesting thoughts there. This is going to take place at the end of the Tribulation Period. We read, *"The burden of the word of the Lord for Israel, saith the Lord, which stretcheth forth the heavens, and layeth the foundation of the earth, and formeth the spirit of man within him. Behold, I will make Jerusalem a cup of trembling unto all the people round about, when they shall be in the siege both against Judah and against Jerusalem. And in that day will I make Jerusalem a burdensome stone for all people: all that burden themselves with it shall be cut in pieces, though all the people of the earth be gathered together against it"* (Zech. 12: 1-3). This is something that God has indicated will take place in the future. It has not yet been fulfilled. This will be fulfilled during what is called the time of Jacob's trouble.

In Zechariah 12:10 we read, "... *and they shall look upon me whom they have pierced, and they shall mourn for him, as one mourneth for his only son, and shall be in bitterness for him, as one that is in bitterness for his firstborn."* That is the time, I believe, when Israel as a nation is going to come to a place where they will accept Christ as their Savior.

Rob Lindsted: So that is really *in* the Tribulation Period.

Earl Warner: Yes.

Rob Lindsted: So what we have then is a distinction. When we talk about the second coming of Christ we really must divide it into two parts. Those two parts are seven years apart. The first part is when He comes *for* believers. Those that are dead are going to meet Christ in the clouds in a new body. 1 Thessalonians 4:17 says, *"Then we which are alive and remain shall be caught up together with them in the clouds to meet the Lord in the air: and so shall we ever be with the Lord."* So this is the first aspect of the second coming of Christ.

But then what we find is seven years later Christ is going to come back to the earth. As He comes back to the earth, He is going to be coming back *with* those that are believers. So we find a great contrast. One aspect of the second coming of Christ is as He comes back in the clouds; another is as He comes back to the earth. In one He comes back to take a bride; in the other He comes back to set up a kingdom. So there really are some very distinct differences. But what you are saying is that there is something very important that happens, especially for Jewish people in this period of seven years between the first and the second aspects of the coming of Christ. Based on Zechariah this is when Jesus will reveal Himself to the Jewish people.

Earl Warner: Amen. Jeremiah 30:7 indicates that it is going to be a time of great trouble when all the nations of the world are going to come against Israel and Israel will have no help, no hope. In fact, Zechariah 13:8-9 says that two-thirds of the Jewish people in Israel are going to be destroyed, they are going to be massacred like cattle. And God is going to come down and fight for them. In fact, in the last three great biblical wars we find no evidence that Israel is going to fire even one shot. God is going to do it. In Revelation 19 we find that at the end of the Tribulation Period, God is going to come down and He is going to do the fighting. In fact, in Zechariah 14:3 we read, *"Then shall the Lord go forth, and fight against those nations, as when he fought in the day of battle."* This indicates that the Lord is going to come down and fight against those who come against Israel. We read in verse 4 that in that day, as people stand on the Mount of Olives, it will be split in two from east to west. Then in the latter part of verse 5 we read, *". . . and the Lord my God shall come, and all the saints with thee"* exactly what we read in Revelation 19. Of course if we are going to come back with Him, we have to go up first. So we are going to go up first at the Rapture of the Church, and then we are going to come back with Him and rule and reign with Him for the period of time when He is on earth. This really rejoices my heart.

I have no doubt that the Lord Jesus Christ is the Messiah of whom Moses and all of the prophets have written. Even though I made that decision to accept Him many years ago, I know it is the greatest decision I ever made. I will never reject Him as my Savior because I know He is the one of whom Moses and the prophets have written. What a wonderful truth.

Rob Lindsted: As you have pointed out, in Zechariah 12:10 it is such a clear statement that there is going to come a day that they who pierced Him are going to look upon Him with sorrow. That must be the Jewish people. They are going to have to acknowledge Him for who He is, the great Messiah, the great Savior of the world. What an exciting time.

The Rapture of the Church is what you and I ought to be looking for: the soon return of Christ in the clouds to take believers. Our prayer today is that every one of our readers are ready for that time, looking forward to that time. The Bible says that we spent this period of time in Heaven at the marriage supper of the Lamb and at the end of that time we will come back to the earth. That is when He will set up His kingdom. I wonder if maybe this isn't why the Jewish people have been so confused. They are looking for Him to come and set up the kingdom.

Earl Warner: There are some orthodox Jewish people today who are waiting for Him to come, even today. In fact, a number of rabbis in Israel are really waiting for the Messiah to come in this year — 1991. It is amazing that these orthodox Jewish people, waiting for the Messiah, believe that He could come this year.

Rob Lindsted: We have been seeing headlines over and over of rabbis saying, "The Messiah is coming soon." Some believe that this is why they need to get various aspects of the tabernacle items ready, so they can welcome the Messiah. I believe that before Christ will come and reveal Himself as Messiah and before the Jews will ever recognize Him as the one who was pierced for them, He is going to come and Rapture the Church. Isn't it wonderful to know that all the signs are pointing to the Millennial reign of Christ, the second aspect of the Second Coming? And yet we have much to look forward to as we look for the first aspect of His coming.

As we look at the Bible it says that God would blind their eyes because of their rejection of Christ. I think we are really seeing this.

Earl Warner: We surely are.

Rob Lindsted: These things that we are talking about have not been fulfilled under a bushel or in a corner. These are signs that dominate headlines. It seems like there would be many Jews coming to Christ, but instead we find that it seems they have blinders on. It appears to me that the blinders will finally be removed after God delivers them, maybe from Russia. Maybe this is when they are going to discover and look upon the one they have pierced and see Him as the Messiah, and they will call unto Him.

Earl Warner: I think that will be the final situation in which Israel will find herself.

Rob Lindsted: There is another great passage in Zechariah 8, and I wonder if this won't be fulfilled as well in a coming day. *"Thus saith the Lord of hosts; In those days it shall come to pass, that ten men shall take hold out of all languages of the nations, even shall take hold of the skirt of him that is a Jew, saying, We will go with you: for we have heard that God is with you"* (v. 23). I find this amazing because today when people find out I am a friend of the Jewish people they tend to put me apart from others. But the Bible says there is going to come a day when people are going to see that God is blessing the Jewish people. I think this is in the Millennium. They are going to grab hold of the Jew and say, "I want to be your friend. I want your God to bless me because I see that God has preserved you." The preservation of Israel really is a marvelous miracle. The very fact that they exist today is a great indicator that we are living in the last days.

Earl Warner: I agree with you 100 percent.

Rob Lindsted: Concerning Christ's Second Coming there is much confusion today about why there is this pause where it seems that people are doubting that Jesus will come. But we are told in the last days there will be scoffers. We have seen this come to new heights as people have anticipated His coming (some even setting dates), and now it seems that those who are really looking for Christ to come day by day are mocked and scorned, but I think this is a biblical position.

Earl Warner: If we were to read 2 Timothy 3, which Paul wrote about nineteen hundred years ago and then read our daily newspaper we would find that what Paul wrote and what we are seeing happen today are one and the same. How long can it be before the Lord comes for His own?

AUGUST WINNIG

DAS
RÖMERZIMMER

DER SCHNEIDER
VON OSTERWYK

GEKÜRZT UND VEREINFACHT FÜR
SCHULE UND SELBSTSTUDIUM

Diese Ausgabe, deren Wortschatz nur
die gebräuchlichsten deutschen Wörter
umfaßt, wurde gekürzt und vereinfacht,
und ist damit den Ansprüchen des
Deutschlernenden auf einer frühen Stu-
fe angepaßt.

Oehler: Grundwortschatz Deutsch (Ernst
Klett Verlag) wurde als Leitfaden be-
nutzt.

Die Erzählungen sind entnommen dem
Band MORGENSTUNDE von August
Winnig.

HERAUSGEBER:

O. Børløs Jensen
Stefan Freund *Dänemark*
Bengt Ahlgren *Norwegen*
Otto Weise *Deutschland*
Ferdinand van Ingen *Holland*
Derek Green *Großbritannien*

Umschlag: Ib Jørgensen
Illustrationen: Oskar Jørgensen

ISBN Dänemark 87 429 7661 8

Gedruckt in Dänemark von Grafisk Institut A·S Kopenhagen
MCMLXXII

AUGUST WINNIG
(1878–1956)

wurde in Blankenburg im Harz geboren. Nachdem er die Volksschule verlassen hatte, ging er in die Lehre als Maurer. Zwölf Jahre lang arbeitete August Winnig als Maurergeselle und zeigte großes Interesse für politische, soziale und wirtschaftliche Fragen. Er wurde aktiver Sozialdemokrat und bekam schnell große Vertrauensposten: 1913 wurde er Vorsitzender des Deutschen Bauarbeiter-Verbandes, 1918 Reichskommissar für Ost- und Westpreußen, 1919 Oberpräsident in Ostpreußen.

Dann geschah eine große Wandlung in seinem Leben. Er wurde aus der sozialistischen Partei (SPD) ausgestoßen, verlor sein Amt als Oberpräsident und ernährte sich als freier Schriftsteller und zeitweise als Lehrer. Seine Interessen änderten sich. Teils konnte er der Entwicklung in der Partei nicht Folge leisten, weshalb er Mitbegründer der »Altsozialisten« wurde; teils bekam für ihn das Christentum eine entscheidende Bedeutung. Winnig hat in seinen autobiographischen Schriften seinen Weg von der Politik zum Christentum geschildert. Auf diesem Gebiet hat er so vieles geleistet, daß er 1953 zum Dr. theol. honoris causa ernannt wurde.

ANDERE WERKE DES AUTORS

Preußischer Kommiß (Erzählungen) 1910. Die ewig grünende Tanne (Novellen) 1927. Wir hüten das Feuer (Aufsätze und Reden) 1931. Europa (Essays) 1937. Wunderbare Welt (Roman) 1938. Das Unbekannte (Erzählung) 1939. Käuze und Schelme (Erzählungen) 1940. In der Höhle (Novelle) 1942. Morgenstunde (Gesammelte Erzählungen) 1958. Mehrere Autobiographien: Frührot 1919. Der weite Weg 1932. Heimkehr 1935. Die Hand Gottes 1938. Das Buch der Wanderschaft 1941. Aus zwanzig Jahren 1948.

Das *Römer*zimmer

das Schloß

Graf Z. wohnte in einem schönen, alten
Schloß, wo ihn viele Menschen besuchten.
Einmal kam ein fremder Herr, der über so
wichtige Dinge mit dem Grafen zu sprechen
hatte, daß sie an einem Tage nicht fertigwer-
den konnten. Deshalb ließ der Graf den
Fremden am Abend nicht fortgehen, sondern
gab ihm ein Zimmer im Schloß, wo er schlafen konnte. Der Herr war damit zufrieden
und ging früh auf sein Zimmer, um sich gut
auszuruhen. Hier fand man ihn am nächsten
Morgen tot im Bett.

---

der Römer, hier: Soldat aus Rom

Natürlich gab das große Unruhe. Ein *Arzt* mußte aus der Stadt geholt werden, die Polizei kam, man mußte alle möglichen Fragen beantworten, bevor der Tote weggebracht werden durfte. Aber damit nicht genug. Alle Menschen in der kleinen Stadt, wo das Schloß

der Arzt

lag, waren sehr beunruhigt. Was hatte dem Manne so plötzlich das Leben genommen? Er war etwa 40 Jahre alt und ein gesunder Mensch. Der Arzt sagte: Herzschlag, da er keinen anderen Grund finden konnte.

Irgendetwas muß ein Arzt ja meinen und schreiben, wenn er über den Tod eines Menschen eine Erklärung abgeben soll. Natürlich hatte er auch daran gedacht, daß der Fremde sich vielleicht selbst das Leben genommen hatte. Aber der Mann hatte seine Reise am Tage vorher so ruhig und natürlich vorbereitet, daß man so etwas gar nicht glauben konnte. Niemand wußte, wie man den plötzlichen Tod erklären sollte, und das gab dem Grafen, sowie den Leuten im Schloß viel zu denken.

Das Schloß liegt ziemlich einsam in der Nähe eines deutschen *Gebirges*. Es ist ein

das Gebirge

sehr altes Haus. Man erzählt, daß der älteste Teil des Hauses zu der Zeit gebaut wurde, als die Römer im Lande waren. Leute, die sich auf diese Dinge verstehen, halten das für möglich. Das Zimmer, von dem hier erzählt wird, lag in diesem alten Teil des Schlosses und wurde darum das Römerzimmer genannt.

Natürlich hatte dies alte Schloß auch sein *Gespenst.*

das Gespenst

Es hatte nichts zu sagen, ob jemand das Gespenst wirklich gesehen hatte. Die Leute im Schloß wußten vom Gespenst zu erzählen und hatten gar keine Lust, es selbst zu treffen.

Sie sprachen von einem Kettenträger, der oft bei Nacht durch die Gänge ging. Einige meinten, der Kettenträger wäre Joseph, der alte Waldarbeiter. Aber die älteren Leute im

7

Schloß waren ganz sicher, daß das nicht richtig sein konnte. »Joseph«, sagten sie, »liegt doch jede Nacht in seinem Bett, und er hat am Tage so viel getrunken, daß er seine müden Beine ausruhen muß.« Nein, von solchen Sachen sollte man sich lieber weghalten.

Als nun der fremde Besucher im Schloß einen so plötzlichen Tod gefunden hatte, sprach man auch wieder vom Kettenträger und glaubte, dies und das zu wissen.

Als etwa sechs Monate nach dem Tode des Fremden vergangen waren, bekam das Schloß wieder Besuch. Diesmal waren es junge Leute, die als Schüler einer *Landwirtschaftsschule* von dem *tüchtigen* Grafen verschiedenes lernen sollten, z. B. wie er seine vielen Hühner pflegte.

Die Schüler und ihre Lehrer kamen mittags an, spazierten am Nachmittag draußen herum und bekamen abends im großen *Saal* ein gutes Essen. Zur Nacht blieben sie auf dem Schloß, und wenn sie auch mehr als zwanzig waren, kriegten sie doch alle ein gu-

---

die Landwirtschaftsschule, eine Schule, wo man lernen kann, ein guter Bauer zu werden
tüchtig ist man, wenn man seine Arbeit gut machen kann
der Saal, ein sehr großes Zimmer

tes Bett. Am nächsten Morgen beim Frühstück fehlte ein Lehrer. Da er nach dem Frühstück, als man auf die Felder hinausgehen wollte, noch nicht gekommen war, suchte man ihn und – fand ihn in seinem Zimmer, dem Römerzimmer, tot im Bett.

Man erzählte es dem Grafen, und er kam sofort. Der Tote lag in demselben Bett, in dem vor einem halben Jahr der Fremde auf so unerklärliche Weise gestorben war.

Der Graf sagte erst kein Wort. Als aber am Nachmittag wieder Arzt und Polizei kamen, erzählte er ihnen alles. Natürlich besah man nun das Zimmer. Die Tür hatte man mit Macht öffnen müssen; die Fenster hatten feste *Läden*, die man nur vom Zimmer aus öffnen konnte. Der Tote lag wie im Schlaf. Wie genau man auch nachsah, man konnte nichts finden, was dem Lehrer das Leben hätte nehmen können.

Der Tote wurde in die Stadt gebracht und von mehreren Ärzten untersucht, aber man fand auch hier nichts.

Einige Zeit, nachdem der Fremde im Römerzimmer gestorben war, hatte sich der Graf langsam wieder beruhigt. Er sagte sich:

---

der Laden, siehe Zeichnung auf Seite 10

der Laden

»Eigentlich habe ich doch gar nichts mit dieser Sache zu tun! Wenn der Fremde am Abend weggereist wäre, dann wäre er sicher auf der Reise oder in einem Hotel gestorben.« Aber nachdem nun auch der Lehrer hier gestorben war, gab ihm eine solche Überlegung keine Ruhe mehr.

Zweimal war jetzt in seinem Hause und in demselben Zimmer das Unerklärliche geschehen. Nun mußten alle, wenn sie von den Todesfällen hörten, an ihn und an sein Schloß denken und meinen, daß der Grund in seinem Hause zu finden wäre.

Der Graf suchte. Ein *Verbrechen* konnte hier nicht geschehen sein; denn Tür und Fenster waren vom Zimmer aus zugemacht. Am Fußboden und an der Decke und an den Wänden war nichts Merkwürdiges zu sehen. Deshalb erklärte der Graf, daß er selber eine Nacht im Zimmer bleiben wollte. Die Gräfin bat ihn, das doch nicht zu tun und lieber das Zimmer nie mehr zu benutzen. Der eine Sohn des Grafen wollte den Platz des Vaters übernehmen. Aber der Graf blieb bei seinem Wort. Er nahm nur ein Buch, seine *Pfeife* und seine *Pistole* mit und ließ sich etwas zu trinken bringen.

So ging er am Abend, eine Stunde vor *Mitternacht*, in das Römerzimmer, wo nur zwei

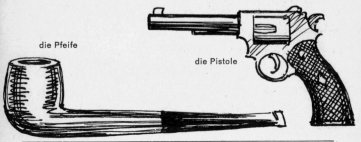

die Pfeife

die Pistole

---

das Verbrechen, eine böse Tat, z. B. ein Mord
die Mitternacht, 24 Uhr

kleine Lichter brannten und wo Tür und Fenster fest zugemacht wurden; alles andere war wie gewöhnlich. Der Graf legte sich nicht schlafen, sondern setzte sich an den Tisch und las, die Pfeife im Mund; dann und wann trank er einen Mundvoll Tee. Die Pistole lag neben dem Buch.

So saß der Graf lange Zeit und nichts geschah. Er hörte den Wind in den großen Bäumen des Schloßgartens, von Zeit zu Zeit hörte er einen seiner Hunde, dann in der Ferne den Nachtschnellzug. Das war ihm alles bekannt.

Um ein Uhr war jemand an der Tür. Der Graf fuhr auf. Es war die Gräfin, die so unruhig war, daß sie nach ihm sehen mußte.

»Wenn ich nicht allein bleiben kann, ohne daß andere hierherkommen, dann ist das Ganze umsonst«, sagte der Graf, und die Gräfin ging wieder. Sonst geschah die Nacht hindurch nichts. Um sieben Uhr stieß der Graf die Fensterläden auf und ließ den Sonnenschein des Sommermorgens ins Zimmer fallen. Der Graf sah sich im Zimmer aufmerksam um – alles war wie gestern. Er nahm seine Pistole, legte sie in die Tasche und ging.

»Man weiß nicht, was man denken soll«, sagte er beim Frühstück.

Das Zimmer wurde nun lange Zeit nicht gebraucht. Man hatte Räume genug für die Gäste, die im Schloß schlafen sollten; man brauchte das Römerzimmer nicht. Aber man sprach davon, sprach mit den anderen im Schloß davon und mit Leuten in der Gegend.

Nun war mehr als ein Jahr vergangen seit dem Tode des Lehrers; da wollte der Graf eine *Jagd* abhalten.

Beim Frühstück im Walde sprach man wieder von dem merkwürdigen Zimmer. Der Graf erzählte davon, wie er eine Nacht hindurch dort gesessen hätte, und wie alles ruhig

die Jagd

verlaufen wäre. Man bemerkte, es wäre nicht
richtig gewesen, daß er am Tisch saß, er hätte
im Bett liegen sollen. Der Graf antwortete,
daß er dann sicher eingeschlafen wäre, aber
er mußte doch wach bleiben, wenn er wissen
wollte, was dort vor sich ging.

»Ich werde das Zimmer für die nächste
Nacht nehmen«, sagte einer der Gäste, ein
kleiner alter Herr, der »der Ambassadeur«

genannt wurde. Andere sagten, auch sie hätten denselben Wunsch, aber der Ambassadeur hatte ihn zuerst ausgesprochen. »Ich habe nichts dagegen,« sagte der Graf. »Aber wir wissen ja noch nicht genau, was im Zimmer vor sich gegangen ist; und wenn der Ambassadeur das Zimmer trotzdem haben will, ist es ganz seine eigene Sache.«

»Das ist doch klar«, antwortete dieser und erklärte, daß er jetzt siebzig Jahre alt sei, und daß es darum nicht so schlimm wäre, wenn er sein Leben lassen sollte, als wenn es einen Jüngeren treffen würde.

Die Jagd verlief gut, und am Abend waren alle froh beisammen. Die Gräfin war zwar dagegen, als sie von dem Wunsch des Ambassadeurs hörte, aber die lustigen Herren wollten nichts davon wissen. Alle gingen mit dem Ambassadeur auf sein Zimmer, sahen, daß Tür und Fensterläden fest zugemacht wurden, und untersuchten die Wände und das Bett. Dann wünschten sie alle dem alten Herrn eine gute Nacht und gingen auf ihre Zimmer oder fuhren in ihren Wagen nach Hause.

Am folgenden Morgen fand man den Ambassadeur tot im Bett liegen, fast genau so wie damals die anderen. Fast genau so, nicht ganz: die rechte Hand lag etwas unnatürlich unter dem zur Seite gewendeten Kopf, die Fingerspitzen berührten den Hals.

Denen, die zum Frühstück kamen, brachte der älteste Sohn des Grafen die traurige Nachricht. Es war ein harter Schlag. Nur wenige setzten sich zu Tisch. Man stand an den Fenstern des Saals und wußte nicht, was man sagen sollte. Da lag das schöne Land in den hellen Farben des Spätsommerlichtes, und darüber zogen weiße Wolken am klaren blauen Himmel; man sah die Schönheit der Natur und hatte hinter sich das Dunkel dessen, was geschehen war. Das machte alle still.

Der Graf stand unbeweglich in dem merkwürdigen Römerzimmer vor dem toten Ambassadeur. Er wartete auf die Ärzte, die schon telefonisch gerufen worden waren. Er sah den Toten an und fragte ihn, ohne die Worte auszusprechen: Was ist geschehen?

Die Ärzte kamen. Der Tote war noch unberührt. Man ließ ihn liegen, ganz so wie er lag, und ging sehr genau zu Werke, um nichts zu übersehen. Auch die Leute von der Polizei trafen bald ein.

»Ich werde Ihnen helfen, wo und wie ich kann«, sagte der Graf.

Man besah alles im Zimmer, auch was

schon früher mehr als einmal besehen worden war. Dann trug man den toten Ambassadeur in einen kleinen Raum und machte Tür und Fenster dort so fest zu, daß niemand da hineinkommen konnte.

Wieder fand man an dem Toten selbst nichts Merkwürdiges. Nur da, wo die Fingerspitzen den Hals berührten, war eine kleine rote Stelle, in deren Mitte man, als man sehr genau nachsah, eine ganz, ganz kleine Öffnung fand.

»Ein *Insektenstich!*« sagten die Ärzte, und doch meinten alle, daß man damit nicht den Grund zu dem plötzlichen Todesfall gefunden hätte.

»Unsere Insekten können keinem Menschen das Leben nehmen!«

So blieb die Frage offen; für den Grafen und seine Familie ein schwerer Schmerz, viel schwerer, als sie es anderen Menschen sagten. Täglich mußten sie an das denken, was hier

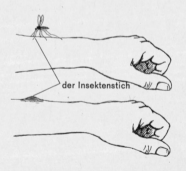

der Insektenstich

geschehen war und was der Grund dafür sein könnte. Keiner wollte mehr in das Römerzimmer hineingehen, und doch gingen sie, wenn kein anderer es wußte, ganz allein ins Zimmer hinein und sahen sich darin um, aber ohne eine Antwort auf ihre vielen Fragen zu bekommen. Auch die Leute im Schloß und die, welche in der Nähe wohnten, machten sich immer wieder ihre Gedanken. Der Kettenträger hatte die Leute nur ängstlich gemacht, nie hatte er ihnen etwas Böses getan. Jetzt gab es also ein neues Gespenst. Nur war es ein böses, das niemand sehen konnte, das aber einem ruhig schlafenden Menschen auf unerklärliche Weise das Leben nahm. Woher kam dieses böse Gespenst, und warum kam es gerade auf dieses Schloß? Was konnte wohl der Grund sein –?

Der Graf hörte diese Fragen nicht, aber er fühlte sie.

Viele Menschen schrieben auch über diese Sache Briefe an den Grafen. Einige fragten, ob sie eine Nacht oder noch länger in dem Zimmer wohnen dürften; viele meinten, daß sie wohl eine Erklärung dafür finden würden, jeder auf seine Art. Manchmal kam auch ein Brief, in dem einer, ohne seinen Namen anzugeben, böse Worte über den Grafen schrieb.

Der Graf wünschte nicht, daß diese fremden Leute ihm helfen sollten. Vielleicht könnte dabei wieder ein Unglück geschehen. Aber
etwas wollte er doch tun; er wollte das Römerzimmer mit einem anderen Zimmer ver-
binden, und darum bestellte er einen *Maurer*,
der die eine Wand des Römerzimmers wegnehmen sollte. Dann wollte man das Zimmer
nicht mehr als Schlafzimmer für fremde Besucher benutzen.

Gerade zu der Zeit, als der Maurer mit dieser Arbeit anfangen sollte, meldete ein *Benediktinerpater*, daß er den Grafen besuchen
wolle.

der Maurer

der Ziegelstein

der Benediktinerpater

Der Pater schrieb, daß er von dem, was im Schloß geschehen war, gehört hatte und nun fühlte, daß er fragen müsse, ob er den Grafen besuchen und das Römerzimmer sehen dürfe. Schon am folgenden Tage kam der Pater im Schloß an. Er war ein ziemlich kleiner Mann von etwa dreißig Jahren. Da er den langen Weg zu Fuß gegangen war, sah er recht müde und *staubig* aus. Der Graf dankte ihm, daß er kommen wollte, und führte ihn selbst auf ein Zimmer, wo sich der Pater schnell waschen und frisch machen konnte. Dann aber

---

staubig, nicht rein

wünschte der Pater, so schnell wie möglich das Römerzimmer zu sehen. Der Graf ging mit ihm. Als der Pater im Zimmer stand, sah er sich nur ein wenig um. Was alle anderen, die einen Grund zu dem Unglück zu finden suchten, genau untersucht hatten, das interessierte den Pater nicht weiter; er fing gleich an, die Wände zu befühlen. Immer, wenn er in der *Tapete* ein kleines Loch fand, machte er es etwas größer, um zu sehen, wie tief es in die Wand hineinging. Der Graf stand dabei, ohne ein Wort zu sagen, aber auch ohne zu verstehen, warum der Pater dies tat. Nach einer halben Stunde sagte der Pater plötzlich: »Jetzt glaube ich, daß ich auf dem richtigen Wege bin! Noch weiß ich nicht, ob ich recht habe, aber wenn man einige Maurer holen könnte, so wird sicher alles klar zutage kommen.« Der Graf stand ganz ruhig und sagte nur, daß gerade einige Maurer im Schloß wären und sofort kommen könnten.

»Dann laßt sie bitte sofort mit *Hammer* und *Meißel* zu mir kommen!« sagte der Pater.

Die Maurer kamen, und der Pater ging mit ihnen an die Arbeit. Auch der Graf war dabei und sah zu, was weiter geschah.

---

die Tapete, das Papier, mit dem man die Wände eines Zimmers bekleidet

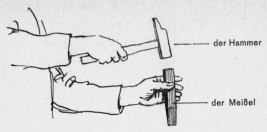

der Hammer

der Meißel

Der Pater hatte ein ziemlich großes und tiefes Loch gefunden und ließ nun die Maurer von beiden Seiten der Wand auf einmal das Loch aushämmern.

Nun konnte der Graf die Frage nicht länger zurückhalten, was der Pater in dem Loch zu finden hoffte.

der Handschuh

»Einen Augenblick!« rief der Pater, der nun mit einem *Handschuh* an seiner einen Hand vor dem Loch stand. »Wir suchen das böse Gespenst, das hier einem Menschen nach dem anderen das Leben genommen hat«; hierbei griff er in die Öffnung. Nach wenigen Sekunden zog er die Hand wieder heraus mit den Worten: »Hier ist es!« In seiner Hand hielt der Pater ein kleines merkwürdiges, farbloses Tier, etwa zehn Zentimeter lang. Es hatte eine Form, die alle an einen *Drachen,* wie sie ihn in den Bilderbüchern ihrer Kinderzeit gesehen hatten, denken ließ.

der Drachen

Der Graf und die Maurer traten vorsichtig näher.

»Ein *Skorpion!*« sagte der Pater. »Der Skorpion ist der Mörder!

Der Graf holte schnell ein Glas herbei. Der Pater ließ den Skorpion in das Glas fallen und legte einen *Ziegelstein* darüber. Man suchte noch weiter, aber in dem Loch fand man nichts mehr.

»Nun wissen wir, warum hier so traurige Dinge geschehen sind«, sagte der Pater. »Ich habe diese Antwort auf alle unsere Fragen er-

der Skorpion

der Ziegelstein, siehe Zeichnung auf Seite 20

wartet; denn ich habe in Montserrat fast das-
selbe erlebt. Dort half uns ein alter Arbeiter,
die richtige Antwort zu finden.«

»Aber wie kann dieses Tier einen Menschen ums Leben bringen?« fragte der Graf.

»Die Frage ist leicht zu beantworten«, sagte der Pater. »Dazu ist sein *Gift* stark genug. Schwerer zu erklären ist, daß es einem schlafenden Menschen das Leben nehmen kann, ohne daß dieser dabei erwacht. Die Toten in Montserrat lagen, als ob sie in Ruhe und Frieden eingeschlafen wären.«

»Genau so war es auch hier«, sagte der Graf. »Sie lagen alle wie in ruhigem Schlaf. Nur der Ambassadeur lag etwas anders, nämlich mit der einen Hand am Hals.«

Der Pater wurde aufmerksam. »Dann haben unsere Ärzte wohl recht; sie meinten, daß ein Skorpion immer eine Stelle findet, von wo das Gift schnell in das *Gehirn* kommen kann. Dadurch macht er den schlafenden Menschen kraftlos.

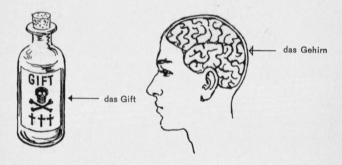

das Gehirn

das Gift

Ob es richtig ist, weiß ich nicht, aber man kennt so etwas auch bei anderen Tieren. Ob und warum es wirklich so zugeht, sind Fragen, die wir vielleicht nie werden beantworten können. Die alten Ägypter glaubten, daß der Skorpion ein himmlisches Tier wäre, wir ha-

das Sternbild: der Skorpion

ben einem *Sternbild* seinen Namen gegeben. Was ist der Grund hierzu? Wir wissen es nicht und werden es wohl nie erfahren.«

Der Pater saß ganz still und sah den Skorpion an. »Nur eins wissen wir: daß dieses merkwürdige Tier heute nicht unser Freund ist; wir müssen mit ihm *kämpfen,* um selbst am Leben zu bleiben, und darum schlagen wir ihn tot, wenn wir können — —«

Und mit diesen Worten ließ der Pater den schweren Ziegelstein auf den Skorpion fallen.

kämpfen, seine Kraft gegen etwas brauchen

Fragen

1. Woher hatte das Römerzimmer seinen Namen?
2. In welchem Teil des Schlosses lag dieses Zimmer?
3. Was geschah im Römerzimmer?
4. Warum wurde man bei dem Todesfall so unruhig?
5. Womit versuchte der Graf sich zu beruhigen?
6. Welche Gespenstergeschichte erzählten die Leute?
7. Was wollten die Schüler auf dem Schloß?
8. Warum war der Graf nach dem Tode des Lehrers noch unruhiger als nach dem ersten Todesfall?
9. Was tat der Graf selbst, um die Wahrheit zu finden?
10. Was wissen wir von dem Herrn, der als dritter im Römerzimmer starb?
11. Was war an der Stellung, die der tote Ambassadeur im Bett einnahm, merkwürdig?
12. Warum glaubte der Pater, daß er den wahren Grund finden könnte?
13. Warum zog der Pater einen Handschuh an?
14. Was machte der Pater mit dem Skorpion?

Der *Schneider* von Osterwyk

Es war einmal ein Schneider in Osterwyk, der war *krumm* und verwachsen. Das war auch der Grund, warum er Schneider geworden war. Einmal mußte der Schneider weit weg, um Geld zu holen, – über zweihundert Mark – das ihm jemand *vererbt* hatte. Er bekam das Geld und machte sich schnell auf den Weg nach Hause.

Der Schneider hatte große Angst, daß man ihm das viele Geld wegnehme. Darum hatte er es nicht wie gewöhnlich in einem *Geldgurt,* sondern er hatte es in seinem *Rucksack*. Dort lag es zusammen mit vielen anderen Dingen. Damit ging er weiter in Richtung Osterwyk.

der krumme Schneider

der Rucksack

der Geldgurt

vererben, nach dem Tod überlassen

das Gasthaus

Ei, lachte der Schneider, als er die Häuser
von Goslar sah, ei, da ist die gute Stadt Goslar, die alte gute! Da werde ich in ein *Gasthaus* gehen und mich bequem ins Bett legen.
Auch soll mir der *Wirt* Wein bringen. Dann
will ich essen und fröhlich sein! Morgen aber
werde ich schnell nach Osterwyk gehen und
gewiß zum Abend dort sein. Ich möchte gerne
wissen, was Veit, der *Lehrling*, in der Zeit,
wo ich nicht zu Hause war, gemacht hat. Ich
werde ihn beim Ohr nehmen und mit ihm
durchs Haus gehen. Er wird schreien und
bitten, doch wird es ihm nicht helfen, denn
ich bin sein *Meister!*

---

der Wirt, der Herr des Gasthauses
der Lehrling, jemand, der eine Arbeit lernt
der Meister, der Lehrling lernt beim Meister eine Arbeit

So dachte der Schneider und freute sich und ging noch schneller. Doch siehe, da kamen zwei Stadtsoldaten aus Goslar mit Pferden auf ihn zu. Der Schneider bekam Angst, aber sagte zu sich, »Warum hast du Angst? Du hast nichts Böses getan!« – und ging den Männern entgegen. Da machten die beiden halt, stiegen von ihren Pferden ab, faßten den Armen an der *Jacke* und banden ihm die Hände mit *Stricken*. Er schrie und sprang und stellte Fragen.

Die Stadtsoldaten lachten nur und *stießen* ihn mit ihren *Lanzen,* daß er laut schrie, dann aber sofort still wurde. Sie setzten sich wie-

die Lanze →

der Strick   die Jacke

---

stießen, von: stoßen; kurz und schnell in eine Richtung bewegen

33

der auf ihre Pferde und fort ging es nach Goslar. Die Pferde liefen schnell und der Schneider mußte springen, um mitzukommen. In Goslar aber führten sie ihn in das *Gefängnis* und warfen ihn in ein *Loch*.

Da lag nun der Schneider und hatte es gar nicht gut. Oh, dachte er, hätte ich doch nie geglaubt, daß es mir so schlecht gehen würde in dieser Stadt! Habe ich *mich* doch auf diese Stadt *gefreut*, auf das warme Bett im Gasthaus und auf den Wein und wollte morgen fröhlich nach Osterwyk gehen. Wie geht es mir nun! Hier liege ich in einem dunklen Loch mit Stricken gebunden, und mein Rucksack ist fort mit dem guten Geld und dem Essen. Wie lange werde ich hier bleiben, und was wird aus meinem Haus? Der Schneider fühlte sich schlecht, und er war traurig. Doch dachte er trotzdem an seinen Lehrling Veit,

das Gefängnis

---

das Loch, enger, dunkler Raum
sich freuen, froh sein

34

die Wiese

der sich über das lange Wegbleiben seines
Meisters freuen und im Hause machen würde,
was er wollte. Er hatte schon immer böse über
diesen Lehrling gedacht, weil der so einen
schönen geraden Körper hatte und seiner so
krumm war. So ging ihm vieles durch den
Kopf, was ihm seine Lage noch schwerer
machte.

Während der Schneider im dunklen Loch
lag, schien draußen die Sonne auf den Wald
und auf die grünen *Wiesen*, wo die Kinder
spielten. Und als es dunkel war, sah man die
Sterne am Himmel, und dann kam der Mond
über den Berg und schien auf die schlafende
Erde. Als wäre alles so wie immer, ging es
weiter auf der Welt, und keiner dachte an
den armen Schneider, zu dem kein Licht und
kein *Ton* von draußen kam.

Aber eines Tages ging die Tür des Gefäng-

---

der Ton, das, was wir hören

nisses auf, und man führte den Schneider vor den *Richter*.

Nun muß man sagen, warum der Schneider gefangen worden war. Ein junger Mann war auf Reisen erschlagen und *beraubt* worden. Man hatte den Toten vor der Stadt gefunden und überall nach dem Mörder gesucht. Alle Städte um Goslar hatten ihre Soldaten geschickt, denn sie wollten helfen, den Mörder zu finden und freuten sich darauf, ihn *bestrafen* zu können. Den Stadtsoldaten von Goslar aber war der Schneider in die Finger gelaufen, und sie hatten ihn schnell gefangen. Wahrscheinlich wäre der Schneider bald wieder freigelassen worden, wenn man nicht das viele Geld in seinem Rucksack gefunden hätte. Als man das sah, war man sich sofort darüber klar, daß man den richtigen gefunden habe. Der Schneider sagte, das sei falsch und erzählte, woher er sein Geld bekommen habe. Man hörte sich das an, machte sich aber keine *Mühe* herauszufinden, ob das wahr

---

der Richter, jemand, der sagt, ob das, was man getan hat, böse war oder nicht

berauben, etwas gewaltsam wegnehmen

bestrafen, jemandem eine Strafe geben

die Mühe, die große Arbeit

sei oder nicht. Sei es, daß man gar nichts tat, oder daß das, was man herausfand, nicht positiv genug war, ihn freizulassen, kurz, man begann den Schneider zu *foltern*. Das war auch für einen Schneider zu viel, und als man ihm die *glühende Zange* auf die Haut setzte, sagte er, er habe den jungen Mann getötet und ihm das Geld weggenommen. Dann ließ man ihn in Ruhe, gab ihm etwas zu essen und sagte ihm, daß er bald *durch das Schwert hingerichtet* werden sollte.

Als der Schneider das hörte, war er sehr traurig. Aber tief in seinem Inneren glaubte er doch noch daran, daß alles gut werden würde, wie alle, die kurz vor ihrer letzten Stunde stehen.

Eines Tages kommt der *Henker* zu ihm und

die Zange

← der Henker

durch das Schwert hinrichten

foltern, einem Menschen Schmerzen bereiten, damit er sagt, was er getan hat
glühend, durch Feuer sehr heiß sein

sagt: »Guten Morgen, Schneider; heute soll es sein«, zieht ihn aus dem Loch in den helleren *Gang* und sieht ihn an. *Kratzt sich* dann *hinter dem Ohr* und greift dem Schneider ins

der Gang

sich hinter dem Ohr kratzen

Genick. Doch der hatte gar keines. Sein Kopf saß glatt auf dem *Rumpf,* und die *Schultern* waren so hoch gewachsen, daß auch die dünne Linie zwischen Kopf und Rumpf fast nicht zu sehen war. Da lacht der Henker und ruft:

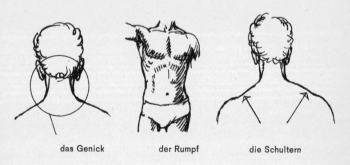

das Genick

der Rumpf

die Schultern

»Dich soll der *Teufel köpfen!* Ich kann es nicht!«

»Geht es wirklich nicht?« fragte der Schneider. »Hätte ich einen *Spiegel,* so müßtest du hineinsehen und solltest mir dann sagen, wie ich dich köpfen könnte!«

Der Schneider wußte nicht, wie ihm geschah und ob er darüber fröhlich oder traurig sein sollte. Der Henker hatte ihn noch genauer angesehen und angefaßt und sagte zuletzt: »Dich kann man nicht töten, Schneider, nicht durch Köpfen und nicht durch *Hängen,* und anders dürfen wir dich nicht töten.«

Dann brachte er den Schneider ins Loch zurück und erzählte dem *Stadtrat,* wie die Sache stand. Es war wirklich so, wie der Henker gesagt hatte. Die Stadt durfte nur köpfen

der Teufel

der Spiegel

---

köpfen, mit dem Schwert den Kopf abschlagen
hängen, durch den Strick töten
der Stadtrat, die Menschen, die die Politik einer Stadt machen

und hängen lassen. Sie war damit immer *zu-frieden* gewesen und keiner hatte geglaubt, daß dies einmal nicht so sein sollte.

Der Schneider wurde vor den Rat geführt, mußte die Kleider vom Körper nehmen und sich besehen und befühlen lassen. Auch den Arzt holte man herbei, daß er den Schneider ansehe. Der sagte aber nur, daß er wohl dazu da sei, Kranke gesund zu machen, aber nicht, um Menschen zu töten. Doch der Rat verstand nun auch, daß der Henker recht hatte und sie den Schneider nicht auf gewöhnliche Art töten konnten.

Da wußte der Rat nicht mehr, was er machen sollte. Den *Kaiser* fragen, das wollten sie nicht, weil das zuviel Zeit kostete. Den Schneider töten, ohne daß sie es durften, wollten sie auch nicht, da die *Nachbarstädte* dies dem Kaiser gesagt hätten. Dann hätte die Stadt Goslar gar keine Mörder mehr hinrich-

der Kaiser

---

zufrieden sein, nichts anderes wollen
die Nachbarstadt, die nächste Stadt

ten dürfen. Zum Schluß dachte man an eine der Nachbarstädte, wo man Verbrecher auch *ertränken* und *verbrennen* durfte. Eine solche Stadt war Hildesheim.

Man schrieb an den Rat von Hildesheim, ob sie den Schneider haben wollten. In Hildesheim freuten sie sich sehr darüber, nur hatten sie gerade keine Zeit. Sie sagten, daß sie den Schneider verbrennen wollten, weil das die geringste Mühe mache. Nur, wie gesagt, jetzt hätten sie keine Zeit. Aber später im Jahr würden sie es gerne tun, und bis dahin sollte der Schneider in Goslar bleiben.

Die in Goslar wollten aber nicht, daß der Schneider ihnen noch mehr Zeit und Geld koste, und sie fragten einen hohen Herrn, der nahe bei Goslar wohnte, ob er den Schneider nehme, wenn er mit ihm machen dürfe, was er wolle. Dieser hohe Herr war der Herr von Asseburg, ein böser und schlechter Mensch, der der Stadt und vielen anderen schon genug *geschadet* hatte. Die Stadt hatte gerade ihn gefragt, weil sie hoffte, daß er sie dann in Ruhe lassen würde.

---

ertränken, einen Menschen so lange unter Wasser halten, bis er tot ist
verbrennen, durch Feuer töten
schaden, jemandem Schlechtes antun

Der Herr von Asseburg wollte den Schneider gerne haben, nicht um ihn zu töten, sondern um ihn zu Geld zu machen. Er wollte ihn an den Vater des getöteten und beraubten jungen Mannes verkaufen. Darum freute er sich sehr und machte sich bald mit ein paar *Knechten* auf den Weg, um den Schneider zu holen.

Nun aber fürchteten die Hildesheimer, der Schneider könnte ihnen verloren gehen und schickten auch zwei Knechte. Die Knechte aus Hildesheim waren um einige Stunden schneller als die aus Asseburg, nahmen den Schneider und banden ihn an einen Strick. Dann setzten sie sich auf ihre Pferde und ließen den Schneider vor sich herlaufen in Richtung Hildesheim.

Kaum waren sie aus der Stadt hinaus, da kamen die Knechte aus Asseburg. Als sie hörten, daß der Schneider schon auf dem Weg nach Hildesheim sei, *wendeten* sie ihre Pferde und *ritten* nach *Norden*.

Bald sahen sie die Knechte aus Hildesheim

---

der Knecht, ein Mann, der für einen Herrn arbeitet
wenden, in eine andere Richtung bringen
ritten, von: reiten; sich auf einem Pferd fortbewegen
der Norden, Himmelsrichtung

und stellten sich ihnen in den Weg. Die anderen aber gaben den Schneider nicht her, auch waren es starke Männer, die *Brustharnische* und ein festes *Lederwams* trugen, während die Asseburger solche Dinge nicht hatten. Sie sagten deswegen, solange sie den Schneider hätten, gehöre er dem Rat von Hildesheim, und sie würden ihn nur aus der Hand geben, wenn es der Rat bestimmte. »Hoho!« rief der Asseburger, »ich werde euch schon helfen!« und versuchte dem Knecht, der den Schneider hielt, den Strick aus der Hand zu nehmen. Da kam der zweite Knecht hinzu und stieß ihm die Lanze in die Seite. Hei! da fiel der Asseburger hin, sagte etwas zu seinen beiden Männern, und alle drei ritten mit ihren Lanzen gegen die Knechte. Da es nun ernst wurde, mußte der Knecht den Schneider loslassen und sein Schwert nehmen.

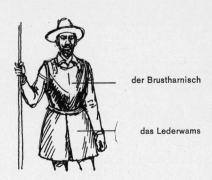

der Brustharnisch

das Lederwams

Der Schneider *duckte sich* in die *Ackerfurche* und sah den Männern zu. Sie schlugen sich und kamen dabei immer mehr von der Stelle weg, wo der Schneider war. Als er das merkte, hob er den Kopf, sprang auf und lief davon.

Die Knechte kämpften hart und sahen nicht, wie der Schneider davonsprang und über die Wiese bis zum nahen Wald lief. Bald hatten die Hildesheimer genug und machten sich davon.

Da lachte der Asseburger und sagte zu seinen Knechten: »Den Schneider werden wir nicht mehr kriegen, ich sah ihn wie einen *Floh* über die Wiese *hüpfen*. Doch wollen wir sehen, was unsere Reise sonst noch bringt!« Damit ritten sie in Richtung Goslar, und als sie kurz vor der Stadt einen *Marktwagen* sahen, *raubten* sie ihn *aus*.

sich ducken   die Ackerfurche

---

hüpfen, leicht springen
einen Wagen ausrauben, alles aus einem Wagen stehlen

der Floh   der Marktwagen

Der Schneider hatte das fröhlich beobachtet und holte tief Luft, als er sich allein im Wald sah. Er warf seine Stricke ab und machte sich auf den Weg. Wieder sah er von weitem die Stadt Goslar liegen. Aber da er sie von innen gesehen hatte und ihr Gefängnis kannte, freute er sich nicht und ging um die Stadt herum. Da es *Winter* war und recht kalt, war das Feld leer, und der Schneider kam, ohne gesehen zu werden, an seine Haustür in Osterwyk. Veit öffnete und bekam einen *Schreck*, als er seinen Meister sah. Doch zog er ihn ins Haus hinein, nahm ihn in seine Arme und trug ihn ins Bett. Da war es warm, und Veit stellte zwei *Kerzen* auf, holte Brot und *Käse* und setzte einen Topf Milch da-

die Kerze   der Käse

---

der Winter, die kälteste Zeit des Jahres
der Schreck, plötzliche Angst

neben. Da aß der Schneider und erzählte alles, was ihm geschehen war. Es war schlimm für ihn, noch einmal an all das zu denken und für Veit, all das Schreckliche zu hören. Aber nun lag der Schneider in seinem warmen Bett und war froh, so gut davongekommen zu sein. Und als er Veits geraden Körper ansah, den schönen Hals und die starken Schultern, da freute er sich, daß er so krumm und verwachsen war und sagte tief bewegt: »Wie gut war es von Gott, mich so krumm wachsen zu lassen! Wer nicht geköpft oder gehängt werden kann, der mag wohl Grund haben, Gott zu danken.«

Fragen

1. Wie sah der Körper des Schneiders aus?

2. Wieviel Geld bekam der Schneider?

3. In welcher Stadt wurde er gefangen?

4. Warum wurde er gefangen?

5. Warum sagte der Schneider, daß er den jungen Mann getötet habe?

6. Warum konnte man ihn nicht hängen und nicht köpfen?

7. In welcher Stadt sollte er verbrannt werden?

8. Warum wollte der Asseburger den Schneider gerne haben?

9. Wie kam der Schneider frei?

10. Was machte Veit, als der Schneider nach Hause kam?